The Strength to
Face the Day

Tear Down
the Walls

Don't Go By the
Way of the River

Charles E. Garrison

A Trilogy of Poetry for the Future

A Trilogy of Poetry for the Future. © 2021 Charles E. Garrison.

All rights reserved. Except as permitted under the U.S. Copyright Act of 1976, no part of this publication may be reproduced, distributed, or transmitted in any form or by any means, or stored in a database or retrieval system, without the prior written permission of the publisher: Grace Impact Publishing, LLC. New Orleans, LA.
Published by: Grace Impact Publishing, LLC New Orleans, LA www.GIPublishing.com Info@GIPublishing.com

This book is a memoir. It reflects the author's present recollections of experiences over time. Some names and characteristics have been changed, some events have been compressed, and some dialogue has been recreated.

ISBN: 978-0-578-88606

A Trilogy of Poetry for the Future / Charles E. Garrison
Nonfiction-African American
Biography & Autobiography / Religious
Memoirs

Charles E. Garrison
A POET of New Orleans
3711 Franklin Avenue New Orleans, LA 70122
Website: **www.POETGARRISON.net**

Published in New Orleans, LA
Printed in the United States of America

A Dedication and Tribute

This book is dedicated to my grandchildren Chelsea, Madison, Kass Noah and generations yet to come. May this always be a message of direction and hope for the future.

"A Trilogy of Poetry for the Future" is also dedicated to my father, Leroy Garrison, a dear friend Ms. Veronica Thomas, and Jeopardy host Alex Trebeck. Each of these people had a tremendous impact on my life and battled cancer to the finish. Thank you for your love, insight and impact which has given us hope for the future.

Table of Contents

Introduction   5

Chapter 1: Education and Inspiration   6

The Strength to Face the Day   8

Chapter 2: Katrina Tore down the Walls   9

Tear down the Walls   10

Chapter 3: Going Away from the River   11

Don't Go by the Way of the River   12

INTRODUCTION

We've been looking forward to the future, not realizing that the future is now. Once, we looked forward to 2020, and now it is the past. What's important for all of us now is to understand that we cannot let fear freeze us! We need to learn from the past, maximize the present, and embrace the future with Faith, Hope, and Charity, more commonly called Love.

My lifelong friend and life coach Irvin Blackburn often quotes Nike: "Just do it!" A Trilogy of Poetry for the Future is long overdue. Just like the website, the CD's, or the book "A Few Gems," so here it is.

In 2016, The Spirit of Almighty God (Yahweh) led me to put together the book A Trilogy of Poetry for the Future, containing the poems "The Strength to Face the Day," "Tear Down the Walls," and "Don't Go by the Way of the River." All three of these poems carry a powerful message. Each one has spoken a life message individually.

People from around the world have affirmed the blessings that these poems have, which gives the Hallelu Yah!!! praise. This praise universally recognizes the monotheistic God of creation, Yahweh, as being worthy to receive name-brand praise!!! Not just praise to His title; He is LORD; He is GOD—but glory and praise to His holy Name, Yahweh.

The poetry is a blessing, and what do we do with a blessing? First, we BOGO, and then we GOGO!

> BOGO: Be One, Get One
> GOGO: Give One, Get One

CHAPTER 1

EDUCATION & INSPIRATION

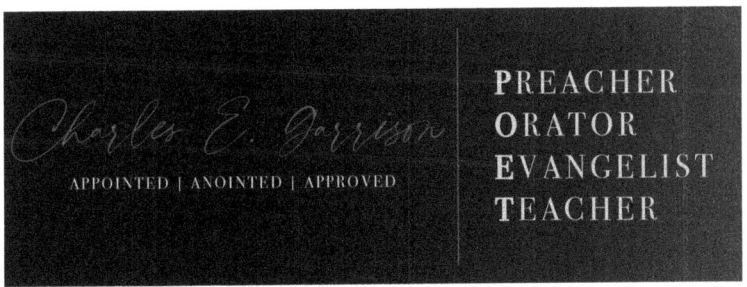

As a poet of New Orleans, I am blessed to be alive! Last year, I turned 70 years young, I celebrated the 20-year anniversary of my travels to Africa, and I met Tamu & Eldred. Additionally, 2020 marked 20 years since the death of the teacher that inspired the writing of the first poem in A Trilogy of Poetry for the Future, "The Strength to Face the Day."

Ms. Veronica Thomas was an inner-city middle school teacher in New Orleans for nearly 38 years. She taught Language Arts and English with pride and a passion to equip African American students with the tools needed to navigate as a stranger in a strange land. Ms. Thomas was a no-nonsense educator! She realized that she might be that bridge, that human instrument that Almighty God (Yahweh) could use to help young minds reach their maximum potential. Her zeal for teaching struck a chord within me and reminded me of my own personal motto:
If you can read,
You can learn;

If you can learn,
You can earn!

As a teacher in the New Orleans Public School system, Ms. Thomas had history with many of the student's families and felt an obligation to hold them accountable for being the best they could be. Structured learning has always been a foundation for achieving life's goals. The home, the neighborhood, the church, and the school all had a vested interest in the success of our seeds. Please note that though seeds may come from the same kind of tree, they may differ in size, shape, or color. Oak, almond, maple, and pecan trees all have seeds—sometimes called nuts—to continue the lives of trees.

Inner-city schools with generational history have been part of the lifeline of the community. Teachers like Ms. Veronica Thomas, Mr. Charles Brown, Mr. Poree, Mr. Lamar Smith. Dr. & Mrs. Reese, Ms. Veronica Downs-Dorsey, W.D. Harris, Paris Pickett, and Mr. Boseman—even Mr. Richards—often taught siblings or even our parents. They, as well as the principals, assistant principals, coaches, cafeteria workers, and janitors generally lived in the community. Afterschool activities help shape dreams and redirect the extra energy toward something positive. Civic clubs, distributive education, debate clubs, and athletics add skills that help the mind, body, and soul.

One of the links in the chain that binds us was the relationship to the Almighty God, known as Our Father, called "Yahweh" in the Hebrew tongue. So religion, which fosters a development and deepening of that relationship, was an integral part of our lives. It didn't matter your denominational, social, or economic status; you had to honor God. If there was thunder and lightning, the elders would say, "God is speaking" no questions asked.

"Did you say your blessings?"

"Did you say your night prayers?" These were common questions. "Wake up! It's time to go to Sunday school," yes, we're going to bible study, were all a matter of fact and not up for discussion. Prayer service was not uncommon. After all, prayer changes things!

Ms. Veronica Thomas, a woman of constant faith (not just on Sunday), believed the Word that says, "Men ought always to pray and not to faint (Luke 18:1, KJV)." She attended a special event in 1999 at The Way Jesus (Yahshua) Christ Christian Center. Ms. Thomas was blessed by the entire event that Pastor David & Sister Gwiena Patin and The Way hosted, which celebrated the arts with music, dance, and poetry.

She especially enjoyed the poem:
He uses human instruments. After the experience, she came to me and said, "I want that poem to have a custom frame with an African print and a gold frame and emerald green mat and gold beaded inlay. She must have seen my expression as she gave me the

expensive details. "It doesn't matter how much it costs," she said.

When I got it together, she loved the finished product and she paid me generously. She said, "Pray for me. I have 38 years in the school system. I am looking to retire in two years and I just found out that I have brain cancer." We prayed right then.

About six months later, she passed away. One of her fellow teachers at Pierre A. Capdau school told me that every morning before we started our day, Veronica Thomas would get us together and pray. The Spirit of Yahweh (Almighty God) pressed in my spirit that that is where she found:

The Strength to Face the Day

The dawning of a new day
a new day has come my way
Full of joy or sorrow,
I know I cannot say
but whatever be the challenge,
I know that if I pray
I'll have the power that I need
And the strength to face the day

No one knows what a day will bring,
It may be sunshine or it could be rain.
But whatever be the problem
Whatever be the pain
If I sing and if I pray
My Master will give me courage
and the strength to face the day.

So my friend, you too by grace
have a brand new day
Filled with joy or sorrow
and hope for a brighter day.
If you start out singing
and never cease to pray,
Almighty God will give to you
The strength to face the day.

I wrote and titled the poem and shared it during the service at Greater St. Stephen Full Gospel Baptist Church with Elder Debra and Bishop Paul S. Morton. I had no idea of the profound impact she had on my life. Almighty God (Yahweh) has used that poem over the past twenty years plus to encourage people from around the world to have "The Strength to Face the Day."

With the uncertainties of life, we needed divine power to make it through. Events like 9/11, COVID, tornadoes, floods, earthquakes, and bushfires have changed how we deal with others. Most of us react to day-to-day challenges from a subjective perspective. It is important that we sensitize ourselves and become more objective as we view this world we live in. We must realize "there but for the grace of God goes" me.

CHAPTER 2

Katrina Tore Down The Walls

This leads us to the second poem in A Trilogy of Poetry for the Future. In 2005, the United States of America was hit by a Category 3 hurricane. The name Katrina found its way into the history books of destructive, disastrous, deadly storms. Most people who lived in the coastal region are aware of the potential of tropical storms or hurricanes. August 29, 2005, Hurricane Katrina, once a Category 5 wreaked havoc over Louisiana and Mississippi's gulf coast. This storm showed the flaws in the hurricane protections, especially in the Greater New Orleans area. It was estimated that over 80% of the city of New Orleans and St. Bernard Parish were flooded. People from across the country and around the world watched in horror as New Orleans appeared to be living up to the name "The City that Care Forgot!"

Although a slow response initially challenged the soul of people from all walks of life, soon diverse age groups flooded the region with volunteers, youth groups were plentiful, eager, and very hard working, and friends, family members, and church groups organized work forces to make a difference.

What a difference!!! Not only for the area and this storm, but also for people responding to each other's pain. Harvest Church of Riverside is one example. A group of friends who used to just have fun celebrate birthdays by taking trips decided to use their time and resources to address the challenges faced by people after the disaster. In the Pacific Northwest, a non-profit from Vancouver Washington near Portland became the "Forward Edge" of ordinary people doing extraordinary work not only here in this country, but in other countries around the world. Teams from across the country—Iowa, Indiana, Texas, New York, the Carolinas—all helped to bring life to the acronym—Together Everyone Achieves More.

While working with a Forward Edge group at the home of Ms. Irmatine Cowart, who in 2020, had just celebrated her 102nd birthday, I heard this: "These young white people really work hard and you can see the love of God in them." This was shared by a man whose religion was thought to look at whites as devils only. Thus, love covers a multitude of faults. It's easy to look at another person, family, or area in crisis and feel sympathy or to imagine what it must be like, thus demonstrating empathy. However, there is another word that brings life to crisis; this word is compassion. Not just feeling sorry for that situation, but also extending one's self to do something to help relieve the hurt or pain. That is what a team from Idaho did. They left their comfort zone, because they were not just religious, but had a relationship with Christ and saw "when you have done it to the least of these, you've done it to me (Matthew 25:40)."

Many in that region like so many others saw that it's true: God's up to something! That slogan became the theme of a ministry in Oregon. What His plan has been, and is, and will be is that we would be one. We must get past our differences and affirm that we must be one! In order to do this, we must "Tear down the Walls."

Tear Down the Walls

*It's happening on the avenue
and all across our town(s)
people from every walk of life
working to tear it down*

*Down with the walls of prejudice
unfairness based upon race
working together hand and hand
that all can keep the pace*

*Things been done to change our town
for the better or the worse
Some things were done that would make you mad
yes mad enough to curse*

*But it's time to move ahead
to make the wrong things right
to appreciate our differences
without getting in a fight*

*So let's go forth on the avenue
and all across our town(s)
to usher in that Glorious Day
when we all help the walls come down.*

CHAPTER 3

Going Away from the River

As we go through varied experiences, how we react is critical. To justify our actions (or reactions) it is often said, "I'm only human." This is true: before our exposure to the Divine Nature of our Father, the Great Yahweh through His son, "Our Savior the Messiah," the Christ called "Jesus" in the English language and "Yahshua" in the original language, which brings life to Divine purpose for Him (and man) being in the world; to show and say: "Yahweh saves," "Yahweh is salvation," "Mankind is on a path of self-destruction," or "there is a way that seems right unto a man, but the end is death." The third poem in A Trilogy of Poetry for the Future is "Don't go by the way of the River." As I was riding across the Mississippi River Bridge in New Orleans, the Spirit of Almighty God (Yahweh) spoke into my spirit: "That's what's wrong with My people; they have gone by the way of the river!"

Then, like the bridge police, I heard, "Pull over anywhere. Write, "Don't Go by the Way of the River."

Don't Go by the Way of the River

The River, not just any river
The Mississippi River
mighty strong life giver
but something causes a shiver

Why say, Don't Go by the Way of the River
"Can't you see there's a message in me
Don't you know I go with the flow
And even though I sometimes go slow
I pick up trash wherever I go?"

So don't go, please don't go,
Don't Go by the Way of the River
Nature does what nature do
That's the same for me and you

But if by nature we go with the flow
The innocence of nature we'll see no mo'
Moving with current trends
Changing with the times

Overstepping our limits
going past our bounds
Causing pain and destruction
to all those around

So don't go, please don't go,
Don't Go by the Way of the River

How the river ends is not how it began.
The same is true of every woman or man.
Little girls playing, boys having fun
Never imaging they'd be on the run

Running from past mistakes,
or causing some hearts to break;
so please, friend, for Heaven's sake
take time to meditate

And please don't go,
Don't go, please don't go,
Don't Go by the Way of the River.

So now since we have passed the past, and are into what has always been looked at as the future 2020 plus, how will we go down in His-Story?

I froze in the past. This book, along with my book "A Few Gems" could have, would have, and should have been published long ago; but it's for such a time as this.

As we are dealing with climate change and a change of the minds of the people, it's important to have a thermostat mentality rather than a thermometer mindset. Temperature usually recognizes red as hot and blue as cold. One is left on a faucet and the other is right. Have the internal/eternal thermostat of the Spirit of The Living God of Eternity within. His presence will protect you and carry you through difficult days of storms and pandemics of any familial, financial, civic, social, or political pressure and will lead you to His PEACE:

And remember, "When you have Christ in a crisis, the crisis is not yours; it's Christ's."

Hallelu Yah!

www.ingramcontent.com/pod-product-compliance
Lightning Source LLC
Chambersburg PA
CBHW062044290426
44109CB00026B/2726